THE MANAGER'S POCKETBOOK

By John Townsend

Drawings by Phil Hailstone

"Excellent and informative; usable in many ways - to help transfer into practice from a course, to help those who can't or won't attend a course, and to refresh the skills of those who are getting rusty."

David Backhouse, Director, MCS Learning and Professional Development, PricewaterhouseCoopers

CONTENTS

THE MANAGER'S ROLE

MANAGEMENT
DEFINITION

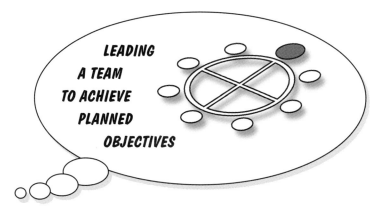

LEADING
A TEAM
TO ACHIEVE
PLANNED
OBJECTIVES

MANAGEMENT

DEFINITION

The word 'management' comes from the French 'manège' (Italian 'maneggio') which means dressage exercises to train horses in obedience and deportment!

MANAGEMENT TASKS

This pocketbook deals with five kinds of tasks which are generic to all management (ie: team leading) jobs.

PLANNING
Mission/Strategy planning
Objective setting

ORGANISING
Organising time
Organising work
Decision-making

LEADING
Setting direction
Aligning the team
Motivating and inspiring

CONTROLLING
Correcting errors
Disciplining
Appraising

ACHIEVING
Putting it all together and getting the right things done

MANAGER V SPECIALIST

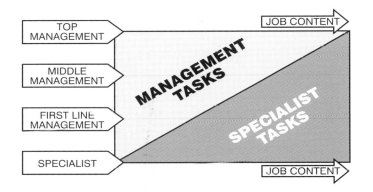

TRANSITION: SPECIALIST TO MANAGER
GOLDEN RULES

The newly-appointed manager

- Re-negotiate previous on-the-job relationships (colleagues, mates, old bosses)

- Don't pass the buck - be loyal to your new boss

- Face the music - you are now the conductor! (It's your POLCA!)

TRANSITION: SPECIALIST TO MANAGER

GOLDEN RULES

The newly-appointed manager's boss

- Communicate the promotion and **all** it's consequences to **all** the team members

- Delegate - don't abdicate!

- Be sensitive to the new manager's role conflict

ROLE CONFLICT (EXERCISE)

Take a few minutes to complete these lists of roles which are often in conflict. What can you do to minimise this conflict?

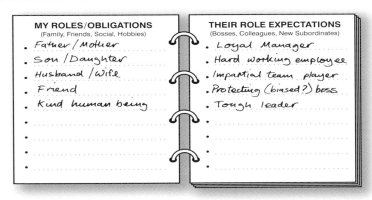

MY ROLES/OBLIGATIONS
(Family, Friends, Social, Hobbies)

- Father / Mother
- Son / Daughter
- Husband / Wife
- Friend
- Kind human being
- ·
- ·
- ·
- ·

THEIR ROLE EXPECTATIONS
(Bosses, Colleagues, New Subordinates)

- Loyal Manager
- Hard working employee
- Impartial team player
- Protecting (biased?) boss
- Tough leader
- ·
- ·
- ·

PLANNING

PRINCIPLES OF PLANNING
ED SODA

All good strategic or operational plans answer the six ED SODA questions:

E *XPERIENCE?*

D *IRECTION?*

S *ITUATION NOW?*

O *UTCOME DESIRED?*

D *EADLINE?*

A *CTION STEPS?*

THE SUPERTANKER SYNDROME

A 500,000 ton supertanker doing 16 knots with its propeller running astern will take 44 minutes and 7 nautical miles to stop!

- Your organisation is like a supertanker. It takes time and resources to stop and/or change direction. First ask 'Where are we coming from and where are we heading at the moment?' (traditions, culture, management style, etc) before fixing your outcomes and your deadlines.

PLANNING

CHECKLIST

EXPERIENCE	Where are we coming from?	• TRADITIONS? • CULTURE/MANAGEMENT STYLE? • RESISTANCE TO CHANGE?
DIRECTION	Where are we heading (if we keep going)?	
SITUATION NOW	Where are we now?	• SPECIFICALLY? • EVIDENCE?
OUTCOME DESIRED	Where do we want to be?	• MISSION? Statement of purpose, vocation, ethic or policy. • OBJECTIVE? Critical difference in expected performance.
DEADLINE	By when do we want to be there?	• SPECIFICALLY?
ACTION STEPS	How will we get there?	• STRATEGY? (options/choice) • SUB-OBJECTIVES? • RESOURCES NEEDED?

• INSUFFICIENT RESOURCES
• UNREALISTIC MISSIONS
• OBJECTIVE

APPLICATIONS

ED SODA is the ideal step-by-step method for strategic and operational planning.
It is a useful checklist approach for formulating mission statements or objectives and
can also be used as a framework for structuring:

MEETINGS   PRESENTATIONS   REPORTS

THE PLANNING CASCADE

MISSION

Voluntarily imprecise statements of

- **Purpose**
- **Overall task**
- **Ethic**
- **Vocation,** or
- **Policy**

of the organisation.

Example:
'To provide excellent service
to our customers.'

STRATEGIES

Conscious choices as to how the mission is to be fulfilled
(eg: operating options, areas of emphasis, decisions
on methods, resources and direction, behavioural
desires and constraints, etc).

Example:
'To improve customer service
**by computerising order
handling and stock control.'**

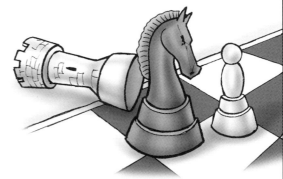

OBJECTIVES

The **critical** few **measurable differences** between performance now and performance expected at the end of a given period.

Example:
'To have reduced the number of
customer complaints on delivery
from the present 10 per month
to max 2 per month by
July 31st without
extra headcount.'

HOW TO SET A GOOD OBJECTIVE

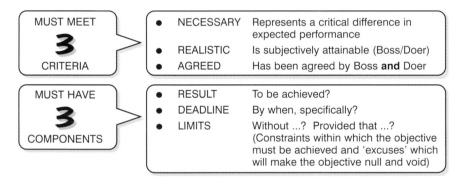

MUST MEET **3** CRITERIA		
•	NECESSARY	Represents a critical difference in expected performance
•	REALISTIC	Is subjectively attainable (Boss/Doer)
•	AGREED	Has been agreed by Boss **and** Doer

MUST HAVE **3** COMPONENTS		
•	RESULT	To be achieved?
•	DEADLINE	By when, specifically?
•	LIMITS	Without ...? Provided that ...? (Constraints within which the objective must be achieved and 'excuses' which will make the objective null and void)

ACTION STEPS = SUB-OBJECTIVES

OBJECTIVES
THE EVIDENCE CHALLENGE

To check whether an objective has been well-formulated, always ask
the Evidence Challenge:

'What will you accept as evidence that you
have succeeded?'

In fact, the answer to this challenge **is** the
objective!

OBJECTIVES

WHY SET OBJECTIVES?

- If you've ever been bowling, imagine what it would be like playing without pins! How long could you keep it up?
- How long would you keep watching a soccer match if there were no goal posts?
- Ever thought of playing golf at night?!

That's really what it's like working with no objectives - demotivating and not much fun!

ORGANISING

ORGANISING

ORGANISING TIME
PRINCIPLES OF TIME PLANNING

1 Define and record your key goals

2 Select appropriate time-planning instruments

3 Identify most useful time savers

4 Get organised!

ORGANISING TIME

❶: DEFINE & RECORD KEY GOALS

In order to define your key goals, first conduct an ED SODA exercise on yourself!

- Where am I coming from?

- Where am I heading (if I keep going?)

- Where am I now?

- Where do I want to be?

- By when do I want to be there?

- How will I get there?

EXPERIENCE?

DIRECTION?

SITUATION NOW?

OUTCOME DESIRED?

DEADLINE?

ACTION STEPS?

ORGANISING TIME

1: DEFINE & RECORD KEY GOALS

E
D
S
O
D
A

THE GOAL FUNNEL
CAREER GOALS
ANNUAL GOALS
MONTHLY GOALS
WEEKLY GOALS
DAILY GOALS

ACTION

The results of your ED SODA exercise will enable you to set up your **Goal Funnel** which, in turn, will allow you to 'concentrate' your daily actions.

ORGANISING TIME

❷: TIME PLANNING INSTRUMENTS

- POCKET/BRIEFCASE
  PLANNER

  - Filofax
  - Time Manager
  - Time System

- DESK DIARY
  (Day per page or week per page)

- DESK TOP CALENDAR
  (Day per page + back of last page)

- WALL PLANNER
  (Year-at-a-glance)

  - Valrex
  - Sasco
  - Modulex

ORGANISING TIME

❷: TIME PLANNING INSTRUMENTS

- THINGS TO DO CHECKLIST
  (included in or separate from planner)

- PC/LAPTOP/HAND-HELD
  (with time planning software)

- POST-IT NOTES
  (with or without wall planner)

ORGANISING TIME

❺: TIMESAVERS (EXERCISE)

In order to identify the most useful timesavers you must first identify your **timestealers**. Rank the following in order of importance to **you**:

- ❏ Too many phone calls
- ❏ Too much to read
- ❏ Too many interruptions
- ❏ Inadequate equipment
- ❏ Too many meetings

- ❏ Indecisive bosses
- ❏ Too much paperwork
- ❏ Incompetent colleagues
- ❏ Too few staff
- ❏ I can't say 'no'!

ORGANISING TIME

❸: TIMESAVERS (IN THE OFFICE)

- Prioritise action items: - A = do now
  - B = do soon
  - C = do later
- Treat all appointments like the dentist (postponing normally means sliding back!)
- Implement a 'quiet hour' with no interruptions
- Never touch a piece of paper more than once! Try it - it works!
- Group appointments together and fix time limits
- Always seek **precise** information from others
- Put time limits on meetings and stick to them

ORGANISING TIME
❺: TIMESAVERS (OUTSIDE THE OFFICE)

- Always have your time planner close at hand
- Use down-time productively (delayed flights, waiting ...)
- Read weekly not daily news (in bus, train or plane)
- Watch TV news every other day
- Get up 30 minutes earlier
- Block hours/days for hobbies
- When in doubt - do it now!

ORGANISING TIME

❸: TIMESAVERS (MEMORY TECHNIQUES)

One way to save time is to improve your memory! Here's a memory technique used by the Romans for remembering a series of things (to do, to say, to buy).

THE **LOCUS** (Place) SYSTEM

- First 'visit' your house/flat or room in a specific sequence of rooms or pieces of furniture

- Decide once and for all that this is the sequence in which you will always mentally visit the place

- Put an exaggerated version or symbol of the items you wish to remember in each of the rooms/places and the memory will trigger when you next 'visit'

ORGANISING TIME

❺: TIMESAVERS (MEMORY TECHNIQUES)

Here's another memory technique for those vital things
you think of while out jogging, in the bath or
in the middle of the night.

THE JACK-IN-THE-BOX

- Your imaginary mental Jack-in-the-box
  holds a big white card for you to write
  messages to yourself. Each time you
  want to remember something important
  but can't make a note of it, take out your
  imaginary mental eraser, rub out any
  previous messages, write a new note
  and shut the box. To remember, just ask
  yourself 'What's on my Jack-in-the-box today?'

ORGANISING TIME

❹: GET ORGANISED!

- As someone once said: 'Today is the first day of the rest of your life', so it's not too late to start getting organised - even if you should really have done something about it before!

- To help you take those first steps, there are a number of action-planning exercises which you might like to complete in the 'Achieving' section. Good luck! (See pages 77 - 88)

ORGANISING WORK

The professional manager organises the work of his or her unit by:

- **Job descriptions** - Which tasks are to be performed by which function?

- **Job specifications** - What kind of person is required to perform each job?

- **Job maps** - Which responsibilities are given to each person and how will that person be judged?

ORGANISING WORK
JOB DESCRIPTIONS

An up-to-date job description for each function helps avoid overlap and duplication of work and should cover at least the following:

- **Accountabilities** - Checklist of duties for which position is accountable

- **Dimensions** - 'Size' of position (ie: sales? budget? subordinates? machines?)

- **Framework** - Organisational location of position (organisation chart)

- **Relationships** - List of internal and external contacts the position requires and their frequency

ORGANISING WORK

JOB SPECIFICATIONS

A job specification for each position describes the kind of person required to perform satisfactorily in terms of these ten measurable criteria:

PERSONAL	1. Presentation, health, age?	
EDUCATION	2. Formal: years/type? 3. Professional training?	
EXPERIENCE	4. Type/amount needed?	
PERSONALITY	5. Type needed for job?	
SKILLS	6. 'People' skills? 7. Equipment?	8. Speaking/writing? 9. Figures/calculations?
$ALARY	10. Salary limits?	

ORGANISING WORK
JOB MAPS

Job descriptions and job specifications are formal and somewhat rigid. A job map is flexible and tailor-made. It should be up-dated with an eraser and a pencil each time something about the job or the job-holder changes. It should cover the four essential **performance** ingredients:

- **Mission**   Why is this person here?
- **Accountabilities** One phrase for each area
- **Standards**   Performance in each area of accountability will be satisfactory when ...
- **Authority limits** How far can the person go in each area of accountability (spending? staffing? resources? etc)

Source: David Gration, Webster University, Geneva.

(See also 'Achieving' section.)

MAKING DECISIONS

THE I.A.B.E.A.D. METHOD

I dentify the real problem
- What is the gap between what is happening and what **should be** happening?

A nalyse possible causes of problem and decide on most likely cause
- Collect evidence **for** and **against** each possible cause. 'Score' each cause.

B rainstorm possible solutions to the problem
- Record all ideas. Don't evaluate them yet. Encourage crazy ideas!

E valuate alternatives and **decide** on the most rational
- Score each solution against criteria (cost, time, etc) and select one with highest score.

A nticipate what could go wrong
- Draw up a **'Plan B'** in case your decision won't work.

D o! Implement your decision
- Who will do what by when? Resources needed?

NOTES

LEADING

LEADERSHIP

Is there such a thing as an ideal leader? Certainly not in terms of personality characteristics. Here is a list of forty adjectives selected from hundreds written by course participants who have been asked over the last five years: 'Describe the best leader you have ever known ...'.

- Courageous
- Intelligent
- Generous
- Competent
- Fair
- Ruthless
- Friendly
- Dynamic
- Decisive
- Sensitive

- Persevering
- Domineering
- Authoritarian
- Charismatic
- Communicative
- Understanding
- Motivating
- Unscrupulous
- Honest
- Caring

- Firm
- Hardworking
- Trusting
- Creative
- Daring
- Supportive
- Collegial
- Consultative
- Hard-nosed
- Assertive

- Aggressive
- Ambitious
- Warm
- Bulldozing
- Analytical
- Arrogant
- Loyal
- Distant
- Determined
- Intuitive

Some you agree with, some you don't. Many are contradictory!

LEADERS' VALUES

Although personality characteristics do not play an important part in whether leaders are respected and followed by their teams, their values and attitudes do.

The ones most often mentioned by members of successful leaders' teams are:

- Integrity: being consistent in one's dealings with people and resources
- Respect for human dignity
- Belief that the effort people provide is directly related to the meaning they derive from their work
- A passion for communicating ideas persuasively

LEADERSHIP ACTIVITIES

After many years of studying what successful leaders actually do, Professor John Kotter of Harvard University has established that they all engage in activities which fall into three categories:

- **Setting direction** (providing the team with a vision/mission and strategies on how to get there)

- **Aligning the team** (so that they may believe in the mission and follow the strategies)

- **Motivating & inspiring team members** (to put meaning into their efforts)

SETTING DIRECTION

Direction setting is not the same as planning. The leader/manager must first set the overall strategic direction for the team and then set about doing or delegating the planning of how to get there.

Direction setting means communicating a vision of how things will look when objectives have been achieved, as well as outlining the strategies to be adopted in order to achieve them - but not the tactics.

Direction setting involves clear communication - both in writing and in presentations - and an ability to simplify and illustrate ideas in a dynamic, attractive and professional way.

SETTING DIRECTION
FORMULATING THE MISSION

Whether they call it the mission, the vision, the credo, the charter, or something else, successful leaders provide the team with its 'spiritual flag'.

In a study* of over 100 successful organisations' mission statements, it was found that the majority showed five characteristics:

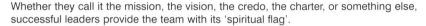

- They were written in a style that reflected the organisation's culture

- They clearly stated the organisation's purpose

- They described the major strategies on 'the way to go'

- They outlined a few key values which the leader wished people to share

- They mentioned several important standards of behaviour expected from and endorsed by team members

*Details published in 'A Sense of Mission' (see Further Reading, page 90)

SETTING DIRECTION

COMMUNICATING THE MISSION

The key to direction setting lies in the leader's ability to
communicate the mission in a clear and precise
way - a way that speaks to the hearts as well
as to the minds of the team members.
This means:

- **Publishing** the key elements of the mission
  in various forms (annual
  reports, posters,
  plastic cards, T-shirts,
  gadgets, etc)

- **Presenting** the mission and
  strategies in conferences,
  meetings and seminars

ALIGNING THE TEAM

Aligning the team means ensuring that everyone is moving in the same direction towards the mission.

Aligning is a day-to-day activity for a leader and involves **communication** in many forms:

- Business presentations to the team
- Meetings with the team
- Face to face questioning and listening sessions with individual members of the team

Aligning also involves adapting one's leadership style to fit the needs and values of the team members. In this way, each person can see and feel **why** they should follow the mission.

ALIGNING THE TEAM

COMMUNICATIONS: THE SENDER/RECEIVER MODEL

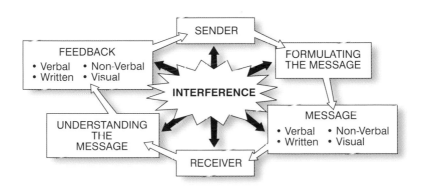

- Interference can and does occur at each stage of the transmission of a message

(47)

ALIGNING THE TEAM

INTERFERENCE

Interference in communication is any distortion, deletion or addition to the leader's message and can happen at the stage of:

- **Sender**   If the leader is incoherent for any reason
- **Formulating**   The leader's opinions, attitudes, beliefs and background will always affect the encoding of a message
- **Message**   If the choice of message type is inadequate; for example, it's difficult to describe a 'spiral' in writing
- **Receiver**   If the team member is unable/unwilling to receive the message for any reason
- **Understanding**   The team members' attitudes, beliefs and background will always affect the understanding of a message
- **Feedback**   If the choice of feedback type is inadequate **or** non-existent

If you haven't received feedback you haven't communicated.

ALIGNING THE TEAM
NON-VERBAL COMMUNICATION

Even if someone decides to say nothing they are still communicating. Sometimes that silence speaks louder than words!

Research has shown that when someone has given a spoken message, only **7%** of the listener's understanding and judgement of that message comes from the words themselves, **38%** from the way in which the message is spoken (accent, tone, inflection, etc) and **55%** from the speaker's body language (posture, facial expressions, eye contact, etc).

ALIGNING THE TEAM

PRESENTATION SKILLS: THE THREE W's

Before making **any** presentation, the manager/leader must prepare the content by asking the Three **W**'s:

W_HY_ am I making this presentation? What will I accept as evidence that it's been a success?

W_HAT_ are my key messages? How can I simplify them? What analogies can I use? What is my vehicle?

W_HO_ will be in the audience? Level? Background? Interest? Time available? Prior knowledge?

ALIGNING THE TEAM

PRESENTATION SKILLS: STRUCTURE

Once the Three W's have been answered, use this 'pilot' model to structure the message:

B *ANG*
- Always start with an attention-getting 'hook'

O *UTLINE*
- Tell 'em what you're gonna tell 'em!

M *ESSAGES*
- Tell 'em - give 3-5 crisp, clear messages

B *RIDGE*
- Ensure that each message is linked to the **audience's** needs/values

E *XAMPLES*
- Give practical examples of **EVERYTHING!**

R *ECAP*
- Tell 'em what you told 'em

B *ANG*
- Finish with a succinct concluding message

* See also *'The Business Presenter's Pocketbook'*

ALIGNING THE TEAM

PRESENTATION SKILLS: VISUAL AIDS

Most visual aids are visual obstacles or visual valium which send the audience to sleep!
Stick to these simple rules for **every** slide or transparency:

F *RAME*
- Use a horizontal frame and logo for **every** one

L *ARGE LETTERS*
- Titles 1 - 2 cms (font size 70-100 points)
  Text 0.5 - 1 cm (font size 20-50 points)

I *MAGES*
- One picture on **every** one

C *OLOUR*
- At least one extra colour on **every** one

K *ISS*
- Keep it short and simple; max 6 lines, max 6 words per line

ALIGNING THE TEAM

MEETINGS

The PARDA 5 MEETING SYSTEM

❶ **P**LAN & PREPARE

5w's

- **W**hy?
- **W**hat?
- **W**ho?
- **W**hen?
- **W**here?

START ON TIME!

❷ **A**GENDA

- List 'W's'
- Number items
- Evidence of Results?
- Get Agreement (before starting)

❸ **R**ULES & ROLES

Decision Making Rules
- Unilateral (Inform)
- Consultation (Consult & Decide)
- Majority (Chair = 2 votes)
- Consensus (100% Commitment)

Rules & Roles for Members
- Time?
- Order?
- Note-taker?
- Scribe?
- Devil's Advocate?
- Facilitator?
- Chairperson?

❺ **A**CTION PLAN

- Agree on summary
- Who will do what by when?
- Next meeting?

FINISH ON TIME!

❹ **D**ISCUSSION/DECISIONS

- Encourage different opinions
- Identify difficulties and obstacles
- Check common understanding
- Listen to all before closing discussion
- Finish (decide/close) on each item

5B's

Bringing-in
Asking for people's opinions by name

Blockbusting
Asking for SPECIFIC information

Blocking
Disagreeing or Interrupting to control process

Boosting
Agreeing, Supporting, Backing up

Building
Adding to (name). Summarising common ground

53

ALIGNING THE TEAM
FACE-TO-FACE: QUESTIONING SKILLS

In order to minimise 'interference' in your communication with the team and to get 'high quality' information which you can use for decision-making (remember the 7%?), you must develop your **Questioning Skills**. These are also vital in interviewing situations. Most managers ask bad questions, get imprecise, bad quality information and then wonder why the decisions they take based on this information often turn out to be bad decisions!! In fact, most questions we ask are:

- **Multiple Questions**   which allow a reply to the last or easiest one!
- **Leading Questions**   which give the answer we want! Example: 'Well, I'm sure you have no major health problems, eh?'

ALIGNING THE TEAM

FACE-TO-FACE: QUESTIONING SKILLS

Closed questions (to which there is only one answer)

- **Probing**
  - How many defects have come off the line this week?
  - What is the sales turnover of XYZ?

- **Blockbusting**
  Noun blockbuster   - Which (noun) specifically?
  Verb blockbuster   - How (verb) exactly?
  Universal blockbuster   - All? .. Never? .. Everyone?
  Comparison blockbuster - Compared to what?

ALIGNING THE TEAM

FACE-TO-FACE: QUESTIONING SKILLS

Open questions (to which there are many possible answers)

- **'About' questions**
  - Tell me more about ...
  - What do you think about ...?

- **Hypothetical**
  - What would you do if ...?
  - Let's role-play this ...
  - What could have happened ...?

- **Challenges**

  Evidence — What will you accept as evidence?

  Missing Link — What info are we missing before ...?

  Devil's Advocate — What counter-arguments can you think of ...?

ALIGNING THE TEAM
FACE-TO-FACE: LISTENING SKILLS

Although we 'learn' to listen on our mother's knee and we spend 45% of our waking lives listening, very few managers have ever been taught to listen.

Managers only spend ± 9% of their time writing (less and less with PCs and electronic mail) yet writing is the most taught of the communication skills.

The most common complaint of subordinates about their manager is:

'He/she never listens ...!'

ALIGNING THE TEAM
FACE-TO-FACE: LISTENING SKILLS

Listening does not mean shutting your mouth and opening your ears! That's **hearing**. Good listeners participate actively in the information exchange. **Active listening** is a skill which consists of **reflecting back to the speaker a statement of what you think you heard**.

Examples:

- If I understand you correctly, you don't believe that ...?
- You seem to feel upset with ...?
- In other words, your main problem is ...?
- You thought perhaps that she was over-reacting?

Active listening allows the speaker to endorse or deny your understanding of their message and, at the same time, shows them that you're interested in what they're saying.

ALIGNING THE TEAM

LEADERSHIP STYLE

Successful leaders adapt their style/approach to their team members' needs for task guidance and psychological support as follows:

Direct
- High need for task guidance
  Low need for support

Coach
- High need for task guidance
  High need for support

Support
- Low need for task guidance
  High need for support

Delegate
- Low need for task guidance
  Low need for support

Based on 'Situational Leadership', P Hersey

MOTIVATING & INSPIRING

THE MOTIVATIONAL MODEL

As a leader, you must use the **incentives** at your disposal to encourage the desired **behaviour** from your team members who are looking to satisfy their own **needs.** According to Abraham Maslow, each 'lower' need must be satisfied before someone feels the next level need.

INCENTIVES →	BEHAVIOUR →	NEEDS
ENCOURAGE PEOPLE TO CHANGE THEIR	IN ORDER TO SATISFY THEIR	SELF-FULFILMENT / ESTEEM / BELONGINGNESS / SECURITY / MATERIAL

- Salary/bonuses, etc
- Recognition/praise
- Promotion
- Special projects
- Fear

- Work hard
- Join a union
- Be punctual
- Do a little 'extra' (overtime, etc)
- Agree with the boss

- To buy 'basics' (car, TV, etc)
- To stop worrying about job security/retirement
- To keep up with the Jones'
- To build a reputation/shine among peers
- To grow and fulfil one's potential

* Motivation is encouraging people to **want** to do what **YOU** want them to do!

MOTIVATING & INSPIRING
MOTIVATOR TEST

On the following page is a questionnaire designed to test your attitudes and beliefs about how people are motivated. It will also allow you to establish your profile as a motivator. Since nobody can motivate anybody to do anything, the test will give you some tips on which incentives to use with which team members, to help them motivate themselves.

The questions and resulting profile are based on the motivational model on page 60.

MOTIVATION TEST

What do you think motivates people to perform well?

This questionnaire has been designed to test your attitudes and beliefs
about motivation. Each of the statements opposite has 5 possible responses:

Strongly Agree	Agree	Don't Agree Don't Disagree	Disagree	Strongly Disagree
+2	+1	0	−1	−2

*On the page opposite, please mark the score which best fits your opinion/belief about each statement.
For example, if you 'strongly agree' that money is really the only way to motivate good performers, mark
+2 in the first box; if you disagree, mark -1, etc. There are no 'right' or 'best' answers so please note
what you truly think and not what you **think** you should think! (Once you've scored all 15 statements,
please look at page 64 for the next step of the test.*

	SCORE
1. Money is really the only way to motivate good performers	
2. Most people will perform better when their managers remind them that they might lose their jobs if they don't work efficiently and help keep the organisation competitive	
3. Whether employees perform well depends very much on their working environment	
4. The feeling of belonging to a group with strong team spirit is a vital factor in human motivation	
5. Individual recognition for above average performance is more important to people than money	
6. Providing a competitive pension plan and good sickness benefits are good ways of motivating most people	
7. Most employees would rather work alone and unaided on a challenging project than in a group	
8. Being able to participate in work-organised social events motivates people to work well	
9. Personal pride in their accomplishments is more important to most people than the congratulations of their boss or colleagues	
10. Generally speaking, employees perform well when they know they are considered to be more skilled than their colleagues at some part of their job	
11. The quality of relationships in informal work groups is important and motivates people to work well	
12. Having their work seen and appreciated by senior management is a major motivator for most people	
13. Most employees would welcome the opportunity to work alone and make decisions without supervision	
14. These days most people are willing to work hard and well simply because they are glad to have a job	
15. Even when people love their work, the only way to motivate them to perform better is to provide them with better tools and equipment	

TEST RESULTS

1 *Please copy your scores for statements 7, 9 and 13 into the first (left) box and total them. Follow the sequence and total each box. When you have your 5 totals (the strengths of your beliefs about human needs and motivation) move to step 2 of the analysis.*

Self-fulfilment			Esteem			Belongingness			Security			Material	
Statement	**Score**		**Statement**	**Score**		**Statement**	**Score**		**Statement**	**Score**		**Statement**	**Score**
7			5			4			2			1	
9			10			8			6			3	
13			12			11			14			15	
Total			Total			Total			Total			Total	

2 *Now plot your total score for each box with an X on the chart below and join them up with straight lines to form a graph*

Score	+6	+5	+4	+3	+2	+1	0	−1	−2	−3	−4	−5	−6
Self-fulfilment													
Esteem													
Belongingness													
Security													
Material													

ACTION

❷ *The graph opposite shows what you think are the most relevant 'needs areas' for the people who work with you. Since **you** cannot motivate them, here are some possible incentives to help them motive themselves*

Self-fulfilment	<ul><li>Project work ● Time for hobbies ● Extra vacation</li><li>Use of company facilities at weekend</li><li>Allow to use hobbies for the benefit of the company</li></ul>
Esteem	<ul><li>Recognition ● Praise ● Bonuses ● Publication of results</li><li>Better office ● Car ● Opportunities to be seen by top management</li><li>Special (visible) perks</li></ul>
Belongingness	<ul><li>Service awards ● 'Honorary' positions ● Club memberships</li><li>Time off for social events ● Meet family</li><li>'Thanks for faithfulness' letters</li></ul>
Security	<ul><li>Guaranteed employment contract ● Pensions ● Stock options</li><li>Private health insurance ● Automatic cost-of-living increases</li></ul>
Material	<ul><li>Salary increase ● Improved working conditions ● Better equipment</li><li>Family care ● Company subsidised housing ● Gifts</li></ul>

MOTIVATING & INSPIRING
DOVETAILING

Here is a very useful analogy to illustrate the motivational process: in carpentry a dovetail is a cleverly cut joint which locks two pieces of wood together without glue. In motivation, dovetailing describes the way in which good managers will seek mutually beneficial objectives. In other words, they actively try and find solutions and action plans which meet their own and their team members' needs and goals.

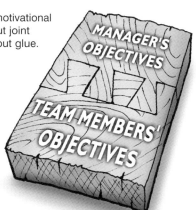

Tip *Instead of trying to 'motivate' one of your staff, ask yourself 'How can we dovetail our objectives?'*

CONTROLLING

CONTROLLING

CONTROL & MOTIVATION

Control is a key management function. A manager **must** know where the team stands against standards and objectives, and whether mistakes are being made or rules broken. However, this works both ways. Working without control is like bowling with a curtain hiding the pins - you hear them fall but you don't know how many you hit or how to improve. The three main types of management control are:

- **Correcting errors**   made by team members through lack of experience, inadequate training, incompetence, laziness, etc

- **Discipline**   team members who have broken the rules of the organisation/team

- **Appraising**   team members' performance against accountabilities, standards and objectives

CORRECTING ERRORS

THE 10 STEPS

PREPARATION

1. Get the facts! When? Which? How often? How important?
2. Never correct a team member in front of others. Select appropriate time/place.

INTERVIEW

3. Concentrate during the interview on the **impact** of their errors.
4. Don't accuse or humiliate. Get the team member's side of the story.
5. Look for the possible causes of the errors - **together**.
6. Show the team member how to improve and offer/give personal help.
7. Set up an improvement action plan and fix a review date.

FOLLOW-UP

8. Review specific performance since the interview.
9. Praise improvement. Discuss any continuing errors.
10. Set new deadline for improvement and fix new review date.

DISCIPLINING

THE FOUR E's

Explain that the discipline interview is to be approached as a 'look into the future'.

Establish the gap between present performance and desired performance. Focus on facts.

Explore the reason for the gap:
- Ask open questions; use Active Listening
- Blockbust vague words

Eliminate the gap:
- Agree on a target
- Fix a review date

CONTROLLING

APPRAISING

CONTROL/REVIEW TIMETABLE

SELF		CONTROL / REVIEW	
JOB MAP	• MISSION • ACCOUNTABILITIES • STANDARDS • AUTHORITY LIMITS	Annually Annually Quarterly Bi-annually	
OBJECTIVES	• PROGRESS	Quarterly	

YOUR TEAM MEMBERS		NEW STAFF	SEASONED STAFF
JOB MAP	• MISSION • ACCOUNTABILITIES • STANDARDS • AUTHORITY LIMITS	Bi-annually Quarterly Monthly Quarterly	Annually Annually Quarterly Bi-annually
OBJECTIVES	• PROGRESS	Monthly	Quarterly
OVERALL PERFORMANCE		Bi-annually	Annually

See pages 17-20 and 36 for Objectives/Job Maps

CONTROLLING

APPRAISING
INCIDENT FILE

However good your memory is, you'll find it very difficult
to remember all the incidents of outstanding and below
average performance of all your team members -
especially if the formal appraisal cycle is once a year.

Create an **Incident File** for yourself (manual or PC)
in which you keep a brief record of those incidents
which will contribute to your overall rating of
each of your team members.

CONTROLLING

APPRAISING

THE APPRAISAL INTERVIEW

The best way to conduct a Performance Appraisal interview is to use the
SOS + 5 approach:

S tandards
- Reconfirm the agreed standards of performance for each accountability

O bjectives
- Reconfirm the agreed objectives for the period

S elf-appraisal
- Encourage the appraisee to self-appraise

1. **Achievements** • Discuss major accomplishments, show appreciation
2. **Limitations** • Establish what prevented the appraisee doing even better
3. **Improvement** • Help appraisee to find ways of improving
4. **Potential** • Agree on the **kind** of future s/he has with the organisation
5. **Development** • Help appraisee find ways of achieving this growth

APPRAISING

INTERVIEW STYLE

There are most probably as many appraisal interview styles as there are appraisers and appraisees. As with your style of leadership, you will adapt your appraisal style to your personality, the situation (good, mediocre or bad performance) and to the appraisee's needs and expectations. Depending on the mix of these factors:

- **Tell**   Listen to the appraisee, then give your judgement
- **Sell**   Listen, then convince the appraisee that your rating is fair
- **Consult**   Ask for the appraisee's self-rating and then search for consensus
- **Join**   Follow the appraisee's own self-rating

CONTROLLING

APPRAISING
INTERVIEW TIPS

- Choose a quiet place and an appropriate time; allow up to 90 minutes
- Ideal 'floor time' = you 40%, appraisee 60%
- Don't rate isolated incidents; use an incident file (page 72)
- Close on each issue before moving on
- Agree on remedial action for each area of inadequate performance
- Use the **Hamburger Technique** (good news/bad news/good news)
- Summarise and give overall rating

NOTES

ACHIEVING

ACHIEVING

SYNTHESIS

Now it's time to put it all together and start doing something!

As Peter Drucker said, 'it's more important to do the right things than to do things right'.

This is the **action planning** part of the pocketbook. To achieve your objectives you first have to set some! The exercises on the following pages will help you.

So get a pen or pencil and start **achieving!**

PERSONAL GOALS

CAREER

Before I retire I want to have:

➤

➤

➤

➤

ACHIEVING

PERSONAL GOALS

ANNUAL/MONTHLY/WEEKLY

My 3 major goals for the year are:

➤

➤

➤

This month of .... I will:

➤

➤

Next week I will:

➤

Tomorrow I will:

➤

MY JOB MAP
MISSION STATEMENT

My mission (purpose, reason for being) within my organisation is to:

➤

ACHIEVING

MY JOB MAP

ACCOUNTABILITY 1

(Maximum one phrase!)

➤

Standards of Performance (to be agreed with boss)
Performance will be satisfactory when:

➤

➤

➤

Authority limits (spending, signing, staffing, etc)

➤

➤

MY JOB MAP

ACCOUNTABILITY 2

(Maximum one phrase!)

>

Standards of Performance (to be agreed with boss)
Performance will be satisfactory when:

>

>

>

Authority limits (spending, signing, staffing, etc)

>

>

ACHIEVING

MY JOB MAP

ACCOUNTABILITY 3

(Maximum one phrase!)

> _____

Standards of Performance (to be agreed with boss)
Performance will be satisfactory when:

> _____

> _____

> _____

Authority limits (spending, signing, staffing, etc)

> _____

> _____

JOB MAPPING ON THE JOB

Now that you've got the hang of job mapping, you should make one for **yourself** and for **each of your team members**, if possible on an A3 sheet folded to A4.

| NAME: _____ | MISSION: _____ | | | | | | |
JOB: _____							
ACCOUNTABILITIES	ACC.1	ACC.2	ACC.3	ACC.4	ACC.5	ACC.6	ACC.7	ACC.8
STANDARDS	• • • • •	• • • • •	• • • • •	• • • • •	• • • • •	• • • • •	• • • • •	• • • • •
AUTHORITY LIMITS	• •	• •	• •	• •	• •	• •	• •	• •

- Use abbreviations and 'shorthand' wherever possible. The document is for use of boss and subordinate only.

ACHIEVING

MY OBJECTIVES

OBJECTIVE 1

➤ To have: (Result)

➤ By: (Deadline)

➤ Without: (Limits)

➤ Provided that:

➤ Evidence of success?

ACHIEVING

MY OBJECTIVES
OBJECTIVE 2

➤ To have: (Result)

➤ By: (Deadline)

➤ Without: (Limits)

➤ Provided that:

➤ Evidence of success?

ACHIEVING

MY OBJECTIVES
OBJECTIVE 3

➤ To have: (Result)

➤ By: (Deadline)

➤ Without: (Limits)

➤ Provided that:

➤ Evidence of success?

* To be continued for you **and** your team on Objective Cards (see Information section).

INFORMATION

INFORMATION

FURTHER READING

'Situational Leadership', Paul Hersey, New York, Warner Books

'What Leaders Really Do', John P. Kotter, Harvard Business School Press

'A Sense of Mission', Andrew Campbell, Marion Devine, David Young, The Economist Books

'Goal Analysis', Robert F. Mager, Kogan Page

'Fine Tune Your Brain', Genie Laborde, Syntony Publications

'Silent Messages', Albert Mehrabian, Wadsworth

'The Interviewer's Pocketbook', John Townsend, Management Pocketbooks

'The Presentations Pocketbook', John Townsend, Management Pocketbooks

'The Trainer's Pocketbook', John Townsend, Management Pocketbooks

NAME: _____ **OBJECTIVE** ☐ ☐

➤ To have _____
_____
_____
_____

➤ By _____ (date)

➤ Without
(constraints) _____
_____
_____

➤ Provided that
(contingencies) _____
_____
_____

➤ Evidence
(of success) _____
_____

SIGNATURE _____

ACTION STEPS	DEADLINE	EVIDENCE OF SUCCESS	✔

About the Author

John Townsend, BA, MA, MCIPD
John is Managing Director of the Master Trainer Institute.
He founded the Institute after 30 years of experience in
international consulting and human resource management
positions in the UK, France, the United States and Switzerland.

From 1978-1984 he was European Director of Executive
Development with GTE in Geneva with training responsibility
for over 800 managers in some 15 countries. Mr Townsend
has published a number of management and professional guides
and regularly contributes articles to leading management and
training journals.

In addition to training trainers, he is also a regular speaker
at conferences and leadership seminars throughout Europe.

Editions: 1st 1989, 2nd 1991, 3rd 1998. Reprinted 1999, 2000, 2002, 2004.

© John Townsend 1989, 1991, 1998.

Contact:
John Townsend can be contacted at:
The Master Trainer Institute, L'Avant Centre, 13 chemin du Levant, Ferney-Voltaire, France
Tel: (33) 450 42 84 16   Fax: (33) 450 40 57 37   Website: www.mt-istitute.com

ORDER FORM

Your details

Name _____

Position _____

Company _____

Address _____

_____

_____

Telephone _____

Facsimile _____

E-mail _____

VAT No. (EC companies) _____

Your Order Ref _____

Please send me:

		No. copies
The _Manager's_	Pocketbook	
The _____	Pocketbook	
The _____	Pocketbook	
The _____	Pocketbook	
The _____	Pocketbook	

Order by Post

MANAGEMENT POCKETBOOKS LTD
LAUREL HOUSE, STATION APPROACH, ALRESFORD,
HAMPSHIRE SO24 9JH UK

Order by Phone, Fax or Internet

Telephone: +44 (0)1962 735573
Facsimile: +44 (0)1962 733637
E-mail: sales@pocketbook.co.uk
Web: www.pocketbook.co.uk

Customers in USA should contact:
Stylus Publishing, LLC, 22883 Quicksilver Drive,
Sterling, VA 20166-2012
Telephone: 703 661 1581 or 800 232 0223
Facsimile: 703 661 1501 E-mail: styluspub@aol.com